Mom

I've Always Wanted to Tell You

Mom

I've Always Wanted to Tell You

CHRONICLE BOOKS

SAN FRANCISCO

ISBN: 978-1-4521-0285-6

Manufactured in China
Designed by Allison Weiner

1 3 5 7 9 10 8 6 4 2

Chronicle Books LLC
680 Second Street
San Francisco, California 94107
www.chroniclebooks.com

Moms know how to chase away monsters. Whenever I was afraid, this is the way you made me feel safe:

Sticks and stones aside, this is something I wish I'd done differently:

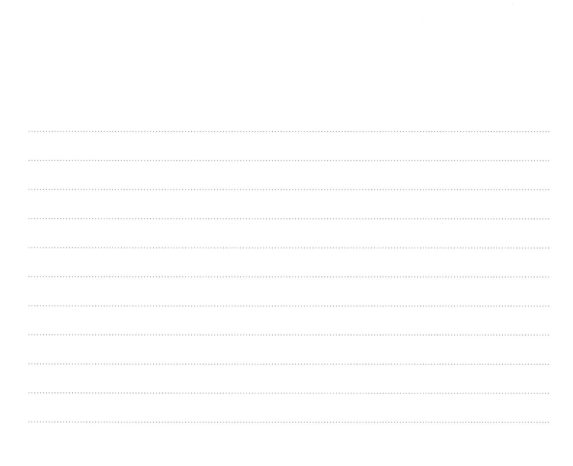

Most mothers are instinctive philosophers.

—HARRIET BEECHER STOWE

Everyone makes mistakes — even me. This is an example of a time when I was wrong and you were right (don't rub it in):

....

....

....

....

....

....

....

....

....

....

Whether or not I take it, your advice is always welcome. Some of the most helpful pearls of wisdom that you've given me are:

....

....

....

....

....

....

....

....

....

....

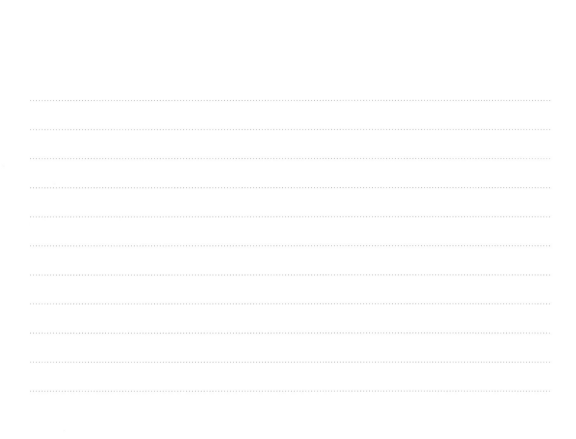

"World's Greatest Mom" doesn't do you justice. If I gave you a personalized mug, here are some sayings it might have on it:

....

....

....

....

....

....

....

....

....

....

You've given me so much —including many of my mannerisms and behaviors. These are a few of our shared personality traits:

....

....

....

....

....

....

....

....

....

Whenever I am hungry for home, these foods transport me back to your kitchen:

....

....

....

....

....

....

....

....

....

....

Out of all of the wonderful presents you've given me, these are the ones I most treasure:

....

....

....

....

....

....

....

....

....

....

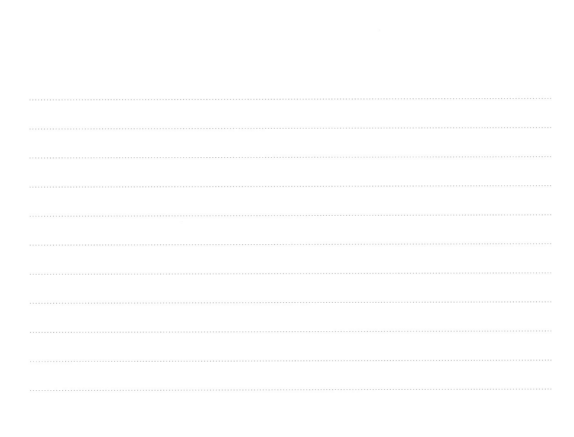

Laughter truly is the best medicine, and you could always crack me up by doing this or saying these things:

....

....

....

....

....

....

....

....

....

....

For the hand that rocks the cradle
Is the hand that rules the world.

—WILLIAM ROSS WALLACE

Tough love can be, well, tough. These are some of the ways that you
tried to keep me out of trouble:

....

....

....

....

....

....

....

....

....

....

Some of the strongest memories are associated with smells. If I had to follow my nose, these are the scents that would lead me back to you:

....

....

....

....

....

....

....

....

....

....

Everyone has secrets. This is one that I've always wanted to share with you:

....

....

....

....

....

....

....

....

....

....

Sweater, n.: garment worn by child when its mother is feeling chilly.

—AMBROSE BIERCE

We agree on many things, but a few things that we will *never* agree on are:

....

....

....

....

....

....

....

....

....

If you had a catchphrase, this is what it would be:

....

....

....

....

....

....

....

....

....

....

Moms are superheroes by nature. If you were a *real* superhero,
though, these would be your superpowers:

....

....

....

....

....

....

....

....

....

A mother is the truest friend we have.

—WASHINGTON IRVING

Leaving home is always an adventure. This is what I recall
about the most memorable trip we ever took:

....

....

....

....

....

....

....

....

....

Great minds really do think alike. Here are some of the things we see eye to eye on:

....

....

....

....

....

....

....

....

....

....

If I could take us on a dream vacation, this is where we would go and what we would do:

....

....

....

....

....

....

....

....

....

....

The mother's heart is the child's schoolroom.

—HENRY WARD BEECHER

We learn so much about each other through the stories we share. This is one of my favorite stories that you tell:

....

....

....

....

....

....

....

....

....

....

Every mother has a mother of her own. These are some of the similarities and differences I see between you and *your* mother:

....

....

....

....

....

....

....

....

....

....

My mother had a great deal of trouble with me, but I think she enjoyed it.

—MARK TWAIN

Sometimes you're everywhere I look—especially in the mirror.

These are some of the physical features we share:

....

....

....

....

....

....

....

....

....

....

Without you, I wouldn't have a birthday to celebrate! These are some of my happiest birthday memories:

....

....

....

....

....

....

....

....

....

....

Among the most important life lessons I've learned is the power of forgiveness. I'll always be grateful that you forgave me for these things:

....

....

....

....

....

....

....

....

....

....

No matter how old a mother is she watches her middle-aged children for signs of improvement.

—FLORIDA SCOTT-MAXWELL

Both of us have our own special ways of doing things. Some of your most endearing quirks are:

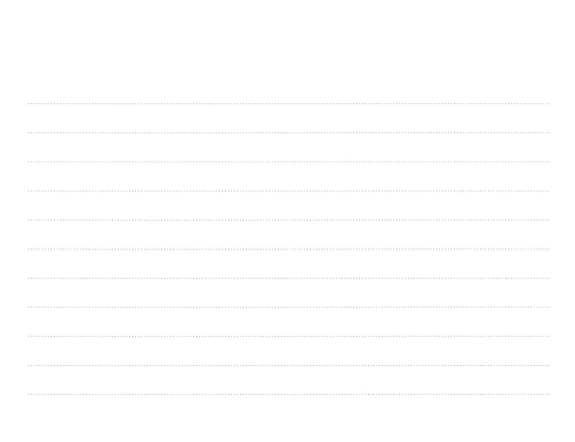

There are countless items from childhood that I cherish. These are some things from your home that I would love to someday have in my home:

....

....

....

....

....

....

....

....

....

....

Life isn't all about work. These are some of my favorite games that we played together:

....

....

....

....

....

....

....

....

....

....

All that I am, my mother made me.

—JOHN QUINCY ADAMS

Music has a way of conjuring up powerful memories. When I hear these songs,
I always think of you:

....

....

....

....

....

....

....

....

....

....

Tricks and treats aside, one of the best things about Halloween is dressing up. Here are some of the crazy costumes that I loved the most:

Holidays are the perfect opportunity to create lasting memories.

Here are some of my favorite holiday traditions:

....

....

....

....

....

....

....

....

....

....

Just like a flower garden, our relationship is something that requires tending. If our relationship came with a set of instructions, it would read:

....

....

....

....

....

....

....

....

....

....

The heart of a mother is a deep abyss at the bottom of which you will always find forgiveness.

—HONORÉ DE BALZAC

You still have lots of tricks up your sleeve. Here are a few of your patented tricks that I would love to learn:

....

....

....

....

....

....

....

....

....

....

Certain scents always remind me of your kitchen.

I absolutely *must* get these recipes from you:

....

....

....

....

....

....

....

....

....

....

Every mother has a wild side. This is the animal that most reminds me of you and why:

A man loves his sweetheart the most, his wife the best, but his mother the longest.

—IRISH PROVERB

In addition to being the best mother in the world, these are the things that you truly do better than anyone else I know:

....

....

....

....

....

....

....

....

....

....

When I close my eyes and think about the time when we were happiest together, this is what I see:

....

....

....

....

....

....

....

....

....

....

There never was a child so lovely but his mother was glad to get him asleep.

—RALPH WALDO EMERSON

I've always been able to count on you to get me out of a tight spot.

Here's one time when you bailed me out of trouble:

....

....

....

....

....

....

....

....

....

....

Being strong doesn't always mean having big muscles. Here are some of the ways that you show your incredible strength:

....

....

....

....

....

....

....

....

....

....

It would be impossible to sum up our family in a few words. Still, when I think about our lives together, these are the first words that spring to mind:

....

....

....

....

....

....

....

....

....

....

If I could time travel back to one moment in our life together, this is when it would be and why:

. . . .

. . . .

. . . .

. . . .

. . . .

. . . .

. . . .

. . . .

. . . .

. . . .

Every beetle is a gazelle in the eyes of its mother.

—MOORISH PROVERB

It might be hard for me to believe, but there was a time before you were my mother. This is my favorite story from when *you* were growing up:

....

....

....

....

....

....

....

....

....

....

You've always helped to shape my views on the world. This is one topic that I know you will always have something to say about and why:

....

....

....

....

....

....

....

....

....

....

A mother is not a person to lean on but a person to make leaning unnecessary.

—DOROTHY CANFIELD FISHER

If I peered into a crystal ball, this is what I would hope to see in your future:

....

....

....

....

....

....

....

....

....

....

If you were elected president, I imagine that these are the first things that you would do:

....

....

....

....

....

....

....

....

....

....

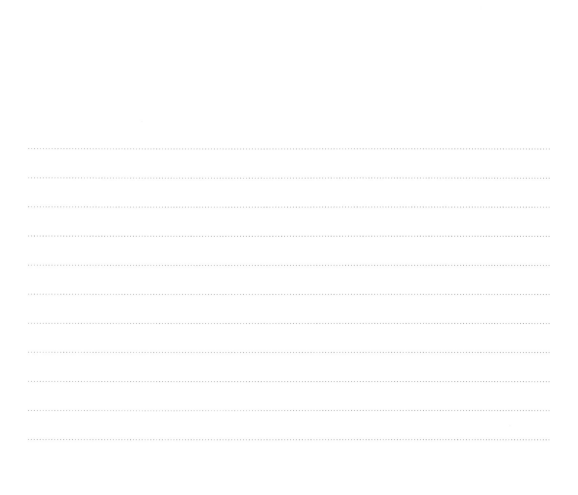

I've never had to look far for inspiration. These are a few examples of things you've done to inspire me:

....

....

....

....

....

....

....

....

....

....

We all have those few indulgences that it would be impossible to live without. These are yours:

....

....

....

....

....

....

....

....

....

Perfect days are hard to come by. If I could give one to you, this is what it would include:

....

....

....

....

....

....

....

....

....

....

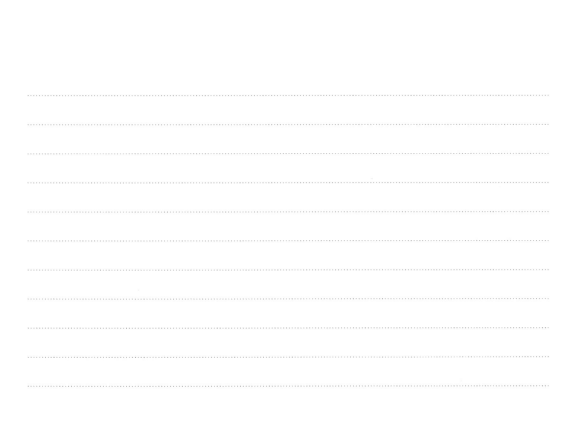

Just because you're a mom doesn't mean that you can't be cool.
These are a few of the reasons why you've still got it:

....

....

....

....

....

....

....

....

....

....

There is only one pretty child in the world, and every mother has it.

—CHINESE PROVERB

Sometimes words aren't necessary. Here are some of the quiet
ways that you show how much you care: